For my beautiful mom

Becomes a Big Brother

An Adoption Story

by Heather S. Lonczak, PhD

Illustrated by
Claudia Variotie

First Edition published on February 2020
POD Version 1.0

Author: Heather S Lonczak
Editor: Heather S Lonczak
Illustrator: Claudia Varjotie
Layout: Andrea Nassisi

ISBN: **978-0-978-60938-2** (Hardcover)
ISBN: **978-0-978-60939-9** (Paperback)
ISBN: **978-1-7344687-6-2** (Ebook)

Library of Congress Control Number: **2020901717**

Published by
IngramSpark®
(La Vergne, Tennessee)

Distributed by
INGRAM®
(La Vergne, Tennessee)

Printed by
Lightning Source®
(On-Demand in a location near you)

Find Heather on Facebook®: @HeatherSLonczakAuthor

Buford and Winnie Barker lived a peaceful life with their 3-year-old son, Gus. Feeling like the center of attention, Gus loved spending time with his family. Although content, Mr. and Mrs. Barker had a sense that one little pup was missing from their family. And Gus yearned for someone to play with besides his parents.

One lovely spring day as Gus was chasing a bug in the yard, his parents ran outside with some exciting news. "Gus, we're adopting a new pup!" they told him. Gus jumped straight-up in the air and danced in circles singing "I'm going to be a big brother!"

Gus's parents were thrilled to see his joy, but also added, "You need to understand one thing, Gus: Adoption takes time. There is a lot of preparation. So, you must be patient." But this news did not dampen Gus's excitement; he'd been asking for a little brother or sister for as long as he could remember— he was elated.

Over the next several months, Winnie and Buford spent a lot of time filling-out adoption forms and emptying their spare room. Gus was busy setting aside his old baby stuff. When he came across his beloved teddy bear, Mr. Fluffypants, he hesitated. "Mommy, do I have to give the new pup *all* of my baby stuff?" he asked. "Of course not, sweetie. Only what you're ready to share," she answered. Gus breathed a sigh of relief as he placed Mr. Fluffypants on his bed with his favorite dinosaur, Iggy.

The family worked as a team to paint the new pup's room. Buford built a crib and bookshelves, Gus placed his baby toys in the toybox, and Winnie added all sorts of finishing touches. When the room was finished, it was beautiful. The family was proud of their achievement.

Gus was beyond excited for his new sibling to arrive. "When is the new pup coming?" he asked his parents more and more often. And the answer was always the same: "We don't know. You need to be patient." Sometimes he asked so often, they got a little irritated. Gus didn't understand that the wait was hard on them too.

One afternoon, a lady from the adoption agency came to the house to meet with the family. The lady's name was Geneviève Peabody, but she said to call her 'Genie.' She was fancy, wearing a hat and pink lipstick. She had tea and biscuits while chatting with Gus's parents. Gus thought she was kind of nosy, asking so many questions!

When Genie asked for a tour of the house, Gus's ears perked-up! "Come and see the pup's new room— I helped paint it!" he said excitedly.

Gus showed Genie the pile of toys he donated, as well as the new furniture, pictures and clothes. "Well, this is just lovely! What a terrific big brother you're going to be," said Genie as Gus beamed.

Before they toured the rest of the house, Genie asked Gus several questions that were just for him, such as: "How do you feel about becoming a big brother? What are you most excited about? Do you have any worries or questions for me?" Gus thought for a moment and then said, "I'm just SO excited to have someone to play with and teach tons of important stuff."

As Gus's face became more serious, he added, "But, what if my parents love the new pup more than me?" Genie looked Gus right in the eye and said, "Well, Mr. Gus, I can plainly see that your parents have *oodles* of love for you. And when we add a new pup to a family, a funny thing happens: The love just grows *even* bigger." Gus sighed happily and gave Genie a big hug.

When Genie's visit was finished and she was heading out the door, Gus said, "Wait, I have one more question: *How much longer until the new pup arrives*??!" Genie smiled and said, "It takes time to find the best match for your family. You need to be patient." "Oh man," whined Gus looking over at his parents, "that's exactly what *they* say."

And so, the wait continued, and everyone got on with their daily lives working, playing, and enjoying family time together.

One afternoon, when he was busy making mud cakes in the yard, Gus's parents called him inside. "Something wonderful has happened!" they exclaimed. "They have matched us with our new pup!" Gus, who was covered in mud from his ears to his feet, shook himself out— getting mud all over his mom. "Is the new pup here?!" he asked eagerly. "Not yet. Come inside and I'll show you," said his mom, wiping mud from her chin.

The family stared at the computer as Winnie said, "Here's your baby brother, Pacco!" "A BROTHER? YAY!" squealed Gus. On the screen was an adorable little puppy with pointy ears and big eyes.

"He's SO cute!" said Gus. "But he's awfully small. Is he okay? Why do his ears stick up like that?" "Pacco is a little on the small side now, but we will make sure has everything he needs to grow healthy and strong," said Buford. "But remember," added Winnie, "Pacco didn't come from my belly like you did. So, he will always be smaller and look a bit different than us, but that's okay. Families come in all shapes and sizes. It's the love that matters." Gus suddenly remembered what Genie told him and stated confidently, "Well, we have plenty of that! Welcome to our family, little brother. I can't wait to meet you."

Buford and Winnie tried to learn as much about Pacco as possible. They found out where he was born and who was taking care of him. They learned that Pacco was three months old, generally healthy, and lived with a bunch of other pups. The family talked about all of the changes Pacco would be going through and brainstormed ways to help him feel more at ease. Gus dashed off to his room and returned with his stuffed bunny, 'Squiggy.' "I want Pacco to have Squiggy because he helps me when I'm sad," said Gus. "Well aren't you a thoughtful brother," said Winnie warmly.

The family decided to send Pacco a care package. They purchased a special blanket which Gus slept with in order to familiarize Pacco with the smell of his new family. They wrapped the blanket and bunny in pretty blue paper, and then added a photo of the family and a special drawing by Gus. Gus loved imagining Pacco looking at the drawing and cuddling with the soft bunny.

Gus knew Pacco would be arriving soon. His parents were reading him story after story about adoption and becoming a big brother. He loved these stories because they answered many of his questions and made him even more excited about meeting Pacco. When Winnie brought home a stuffed animal that looked like Pacco, Gus named his new toy 'Rocco.' The two of them had great fun playacting with Rocco!

When visiting the park, they took extra notice of puppies— which seemed to be everywhere! And Gus's family talked a lot about Pacco and what Gus might expect. They already felt connected to their new pup.

It was July 1st when "Homecoming Day" finally arrived. Gus and his grandparents waited at the airport for Winnie, Buford and Pacco. Grandma wanted to have the whole extended family there to greet Pacco. But Gus's parents thought this would overwhelm Pacco, who would also be jetlagged from the long flight. So, the greeting party was limited to Gus, Granny and Gramps. That was just fine with Gus, who wanted Pacco all to himself.

The Barkers seemed to be the last ones off the plane. Buford was weighed down by bags, but Winnie carried only one small bundle. Gus approached his parents quietly and calmly, like he'd learned from his books. When he got close, he saw a tiny head peeking through the new blanket.

Pacco was looking all around, taking in the crazy scene. His pointy ears darted this way and that, and he seemed to be smelling everything. Gus gently put his hand out toward Pacco and said, "Hello, I'm your big brother." Pacco's face seemed to relax as his eyes stopped on Gus.

Pacco was an unusually calm pup. And he was so curious— especially about food! Pacco's diet was limited before he came home, and now he wanted to try *everything*! At first, they couldn't get him to drink water and were becoming worried, until they realized that Pacco had never tasted cold water before. So, when they offered lukewarm water, Pacco lopped it up!

When his parents held him in their carrier, Pacco reached-out for everything in sight. But what he loved most was the stuffed bunny Gus gave him.
Pacco carried that bunny everywhere.

During those early days, the family was extra careful with Pacco. At first, only Buford and Winnie held him in order to help with bonding. They also took turns sleeping in Pacco's room in case he was scared. Sometimes he had bad dreams, but there was always a parent close by to comfort him.

Gus was nurturing too, like when he gently rubbed cream on Pacco's skin rash. Gus enjoyed this because it soothed Pacco and sometimes made him giggle. Gus was especially good at making Pacco laugh with his silly faces. And when Pacco started laughing, everyone else did too— especially Gus!

Over time, Pacco still looked young for his age, but he was not as tiny. And when Pacco visited his pediatrician, Dr. Julian, everyone was amazed at how much weight he'd gained. Pacco was now perfectly healthy, with clear skin and strong muscles. "Wow! Look at you, you little chowhound!" said Gus, as he tickled Pacco's feet after his exam.

The doctor said Pacco would learn that there was plenty of food to go around, and then he would develop preferences. "Thank goodness," exclaimed Winnie, "otherwise he'll eat us out of house and home!" After the nurse gave Pacco his shots, Gus rubbed Pacco's head saying, "It's okay, little guy."

The doctor was right, Pacco was becoming more finicky about food. However, it seemed he was now getting into everything else! "Hey, that's MINE!" Gus would say with irritation as Pacco grabbed his toys. Gus wasn't used to sharing and found it difficult. His parents reminded him to consider how Pacco must feel, given that he'd never had any toys before.

Gus knew his parents shared most things with each other. But he also noticed that that they had a few things they kept for themselves, like his dad's special coffee mug. This gave him an idea. Gus decided to let Pacco play with some of his toys, but he put his favorites up on the shelf. This made both Gus and Pacco feel better.

On occasion, people would look at Pacco and say things like: "Isn't he adorable!" while ignoring Gus. This hurt Gus's feelings, like maybe he wasn't cute anymore.

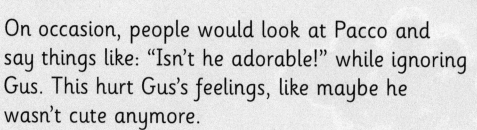

The first time it happened, Gus's mom said, "That happens with all little pups. You wouldn't believe how many compliments *you* had at that age! But the important thing is how you treat others. Remember what Dr. Julian said when you comforted Pacco?" "He said I was an AMAZING big brother!" answered Gus. "That's right," she added, "and *that* is the best type of compliment because it's about the person you are on the inside, in your heart."

Gus still enjoyed special time alone with Winnie or Buford, doing big kid things like playing ball or helping with dinner— which made him feel capable and proud.

They also did many things together as a family; like crafts, visiting the aquarium, and story time.

Gus loved family time, but he also got annoyed when Pacco copied him and followed him around. His parents would say "Pacco does that because he loves you and thinks you're cool." Gus could see that this was true. And, when it got to be too much, he found it helpful to play alone in his room.

Two months after Pacco came home, the family celebrated Gus for being a terrific big brother. Winnie made cupcakes and Pacco presented him with a new triceratops; Gus was delighted! Gus was already thinking about celebrating "Homecoming Day" next July 1st with a big party. Even though he got into *everything* and followed him *everywhere*, Gus had a special love just for Pacco.

The Barkers were their own unique little family who shared all sorts of happy adventures. Occasionally, when they went out together, someone might notice that Pacco looked a little different and say something like: "You two must be best friends!" But Gus would proudly lift his chin and say, "Nope, I'm his *big brother*!"

CABBAGE
~1.00~

About the Author

 Heather S. Lonczak, PhD, is a psychologist, researcher and writer with expertise in youth resilience and socioemotional development. She has published numerous scholarly articles and is an award-winning children's book author. Dr. Lonczak lives in Seattle with her family.

CPSIA information can be obtained
at www.ICGtesting.com
Printed in the USA
LVHW071508190121
676892LV00015B/549